British Values
and a
Preparation
to
Visit Rome

Tom

Paperback: 978-1-968667-60-3
eBook: 978-1-968667-61-0
Library of Congress Control Number: 2025918413

This is a work of nonfiction.

Ordering Information:

Prime Seven Media
518 Landmann St.
Tomah City, WI 54660

Printed in the United States of America

A perspective based on discussions of

    1 Athena

    2 Trajan

    3 Gandhi

In the context of certain statues in London, connected with Rome

    4 A moral compass

    5 Preparation for a visit to Rome

INTRODUCTION

BRITISH VALUES

What makes Britain both a free society and a moral enterprise? That is a question, long ago discussed in the Daily Telegraph-but perhaps it is more interesting to ask, "Who makes Britain free and a society which has a moral enterprise?"

The Big Four

The answer may surprise you - you may never have stopped to gaze at any of these figures. Athena above the portico of the Athenaeum in Waterloo place: The Emperor Trajan by Tower hill Underground station; St Paul on his column among the trees by the Cathedral; and Mahatma Gandhi seated beneath the tree in Tavistock square.

You will say, they aren't British. True, but the values they symbolize have grown in Britain-transplanted, we might say, like seed potatoes, from Greece, Spain, present day Turkey and India.

The Values?

What Values? Athena was the goddess of Social Wisdom; Trajan represented Stoicism; and Gandhi, Soul Force.

What is the connection between Athena and the Parthenon Frieze? Who was her father? What was her role? Who did she disguise herself as when intervening in human affairs?

ATHENA

Which Athena?

The gilded statue above the portico of the Atheneum is Athena -- but which one? Like most of us, she played many parts - but she had the mobility of a bird.

Which Athena is this? Is it Athena Ergane, goddess of crafts? Athena Nike, goddess of Victory? Pallas Athena, goddess of war? Athena Polias, protectress of cities? Or, perhaps, "the goddess of nearness"?

Of all the statues in Waterloo Place, hers is the most interesting — and different from all the others, with the possible exception of one. There`s the high equestrian statue of of king who gave his name to style and extravagance - Edward VII, whose girlfriend gave her name to pubs. There are proconsuls of India, from the days of empire, Lord Clyde and Lord Lawrence and beyond the

Atheneum, the man who restored the Taj Mahal, Lord Curzon. There are two explorers, Captain Scott of the Antarctic, sculpted by his wife, and the discoverer of the North West Passage, Sir John Franklin. Then there's the debonaire sapper general, Burgogne, and, pulling off his glove Air Vice Marshall Parks. Across the road, facing the equestrian statue of Edward VII, stands the sensitive Minister of War, Sidney Herbert and the lady he served, with the lamp. Florence Nightingale stands in front of the guards of the Crimea, in bearskins.

The Goddess of Nearness

The Lady with the lamp may be compared to Athena. Why? Because, first of all, she was near the men in the Crimea, the sick and wounded soldiers that she tended like an angel. She wrote that a nurse was one that could tell the needs of a patient without him having to open his mouth. As we shall see, this was true of Athena, who was a guardian angel to both Achilles and Odysseus - she was right beside them when they needed help. She appeared out of nowhere in the shape of a bird, the icon that represented her on coins was an owl. So it is fascinating that when she was climbing the Acropolis in Athens, Florence Nightingale bought a baby owl from some boys she met there and carried it on her shoulder or in her pocket. This points to the second similarity between Athena and Florence Nightingale: practical or social wisdom. Just as the nurse stressed hygiene and fresh air, designed hospitals on invented pie-charts and statistical analysis - pointing towards the N.H.S., so the goddess attended to the practical needs of her heroes, to washing, dress and food, as well as social viability.

The Twelve Olympians

Behind the gilded statue above the portico of the Atheneum there's a miniature version of the Parthenon Frieze. The original is, controversially, in the British Museum. Who were the Olympians and what do they represent? Athena was one of them and the most interesting - her roles overlapped with those of several others. All together, the twelve Olympians - who came into existence at the time of the Ionian Renaissance in 8OO B.C. - make up our mental D.N.A. - just as, according to Brian Cox, there are "twelve ultimate building blocks", elementary particles, in particle physics. In other words, the twelve deities imagined as a family by Homer symbolize twelve fundamental concepts (qualities or forces) in our mental world. What are they? Or what do Zeus, Poseidon, Hera, Athena, Apollo, Hermes Aphrodite, Ares, Demeter, Artemis, Hephaistos and Dionysos represent? They relate both to the physical world and the mental. Zeus, the thunderer who controlled the clouds, was also god of law, and a phenomenally unfaithful husband whose wife - the goddess of marriage - was phenomenally jealous and nagging. And the others, can you say which was responsible for the sea, for fertility for Eros, for wine? And what about war, craftsmanship, proportion, communications and social wisdom? Which of them can you distinguish on the Parthenon Frieze where they sit watching the Panathenaia - the festival to celebrate the birthday of Athena?

The wrath of Achilles

Who stops at Hyde Park Corner to gaze at the massive bronze statue - to contemplate excellence? Maybe you don't know whose statue it is, let alone what it is an icon of. After the victory of Waterloo, and the defeat of Napoleon in 1815, they naturally wanted to erect a monument to Wellington. But he was still living, and statues were only erected for the dead. So it was decided to let an ancient hero commemorate the greatness of the Duke.

For Richard Westmacott, the idealistic sculptor studying in Rome under Antonio Canova, the answer must have been obvious. Frequently he must have passed, and contemplated like Shelley, the massive statue of Castor and Pollux in Piazza del Quirinale. Maybe at sunset, with the panorama of Rome stretching island out to include the dome of St Peter's. Here stand two perfect human forms, horse tamers holding the reins of their steeds, poised in a trial of strength yet perfect understanding with animal nature.

One of these figures Westmacott imagined to be Achilles, the icon of excellence in Homer's lliad. Why excellent? Because he knew how to excel in action and in speech.

Now? Through his own prowess and divine help - that of Athena. This is illustrated first in the Iliad the story of a few days in the Trojan War- by Athena's intervention to check the anger of her favourite in his quarrel with his superior, Agamemonon. The leader of the Greek expedition to Troy was threatening to seize the "prize of honour" of Achilles, a beautiful girl prisoner of war. Imagine, he loved Briseis and she had become his (patience, feminists!) in recognition of his great military exploits and the bagging of enormous amounts of loot for the Greeks.

Achilles gripped the handle of his great sword, and began to draw it but Athena appeared out of the blue, to do what? Can you imagine? She was, above all, the goddess of social wisdom and she was concerned with her favourite's welfare.

See: "Athena checks the wrath of Achilles.

The Home-coming of Odysseus

Both Achilles & Odysseus followed Agamemnon on the expedition to Troy - can you remember why they went, who was the cause of the ten year war?

Both were favourites of Athena, but whereas Achilles died at Troy and won eternal flame (the reward of arête er excellence), Odysseus left after the fall of Troy and embarked on the journey home (can you remember where he came from?). The journey took ten years. Why? It wasn't simply that he met Calypso on the way and stayed for seven years on her island (so Freud said he wasn't really keen to get back). Things were more complicated, owing to the gods on Olympus who watched all goings on below. Homer begins the Odyssey by singing:

> "Tell me, O Muse, about the versatile man
> who wandered far after sacking live Troy
> and learned from many whose cities he saw

and suffered in his spirit on the sea -
yearning for the safe return of his men;
but they brought down ruin on their own heads,
eating like fools the oxen of Hyperion;
so he put delayed the day of their return."

Poseidon also got his own back on Odysseus, who had killed a son of his, Polyphemous - so as sea god he impeded Odysseus' ships with storms. But Athena helped - first by enabling Telemachus his teenage son to get a grip and then by strengthening & guiding Odysseus himself with his final task of killing the suitors. After Odysseus left Ithaca, a beautiful wife, an aged father & a young son, the trouble started once it was uncertain if he would ever return. Suitors for the hand of Penelope moved in and took over - eating and drinking and sleeping with the maid servants. Penelope promised to choose one of them as her husband once she had finished weaving a shroud for her father in-law, Laertes. She hoped against hope that her husband would come back home.

So Athena, after getting the approval of her father Zeus, flew off to Ithaca. Disguised as an elderly gent, Mentor, she spoke to the teenage Telemachos, first praising him as the spitten image of his father, then instructing him to tell the suitor's where to get off, and finally telling him to set off to get news of his father. This launches the action.

Later, with the return of Odysseus to Ithaca, to the pig farm where his father has been living, Athena went to rejuvenate and direct the actions of Odysseus in facing the suitors. "She breathed vigour into him, and he immediately poised his long spear with a prayer to the daughter of the great Zeus, and threw it. They would have destroyed them all ... if Athena had not checked the whole throng ... and called out to Odysseus: 'Odysseus, hold back! Stop fighting your countrymen in case you incur the wrath of Zeus the thunderer.'"

So, as at the beginning of the Iliad, Athena restrained her favourite - and reminded us that she is the daughter of the god of justice.

The Justice of Athena

How many allegorical figures are there in London that remind us of Athena - feminine figures, of course - some wearing a helmet, all holding a spear or sword, and some a shield and called Britannia? The figures above the entrance to Waterloo Station the goddess of war and responsible for Victory, and the Britannia figure on the pedestal of the statue of Queen Anne in front of St Paul's suggests nationhood. But the more familiar figure of Justice above the Old Bailey - though less resembling the Athena in Waterloo Place represents the essential characteristics from the Athena of Homer who developed into the Athena of Aeschylous. In his tragedy, The Eumenides, 458 B.C., the goddess emerges not only as the voice of social wisdom but as the champion of the jury system. How? Can you remember what happened to Agamemnon after he had led the Greek expedition to Troy and Troy had fallen? What his wife Clytemnestra had got up to while her husband was at Troy, and what she did to him in his bath when he returned? Whereas Odysseus returned in the end to a faithful wife, old maid servant and faithful dog Argus, poor Agamemnon got murdered in his bath by his wife and her lover Aegisthus. This posed a challenge for the son, Orestes who, like Hamlet, felt honour bound to avenge his father's death.

F.W.Pomeroy, *Justice*

He was instructed to take action by Apollo, god of light, but hounded by the ancient Furies whose office it was to protect the sacredness of the blood-tie. Then, by a new dispensation of Zeus, Athena presided over a hearing with a citizen jury at the Areopagus on the Acropolis. So the goddess brings persuasion to bear - she instructs the jury and casts the deciding vote, which acquits Orestes. Then she placates the Furies, whom now become the Eumenides (Kindly Ones) with a new abode on the Areopagus, with a role in the polis instead of the family.

See: "Athena presides over justice"

Athena Polias, goddess of the city

The same year the Eumenides was acted, in 458 B.C., Pericles made his Funeral Speech: Athenians enjoyed liberty and the security of law. Athens was an education to all Hellas - everyone to her festivals and culture. On the Parthenon Frieze there's the festival of thanks-giving and prayer to Athena - the joyful activities of many more than the 20,000 - 25,000 citizens of Athens itself.

Perhaps the best idea we can get of the atmosphere is the opening of the London Olympics. The singing of "Jerusalem" echoed a great imperial past and a kind of spiritual aspiration shared by not only Londoners but many visitors to the city.

In the Parthenon Room of the British Museum it is not, first of all, the Olympian deities that strike us, but the riders in the energetic procession all showing their skill on the way up to the Temple of Athena on the Acropolis. There are athletics contests, dramas, epic poetry, sacrifices, hymns, feasting - so the whole place is transformed for days on end.

All in honour of their patron goddess, Athena - the quiet maiden we see seated to the right of her father Zeus at the centre of the Frieze. Soon the peplos (sacred robe) will be presented to her in her temple.

At the centre of the Eastern Pediment there is a gap between the figures of other deities: here was once Athena stepping out of the head of Zeus, cracked open by the axe of Hephaistos, born to bring reason into the lives of humankind.

The new Parthenon Frieze

As the Taj Mahal was dedicated by a Mogul emperor to a loved wife and the Eleanor Cross was dedicated by Edward I to his wife of that name, so the Albert Memorial was dedicated by Victoria and her people to Prince Albert. We can imagine how important it was to her, as after Alhert's death she dressed in black until her own. It was a memorial of love.

It was also an echo of the ancient Parthenon, as the idea for this shrine of the Prince came from the shrine built in 490 B.C. for Athena. Also, it had a frieze like the original temple, sculpted not with twelve deities but with 169 artistic mentors venerated by the Victeriens.

It takes time for us to get our heads round this monument expert opinions clash over it: Lord Clark called it "pure philistinism" but Gavin Stamp has praised it as the major achievement of the Gothic Renaissance. So it doesn't matter that much what experts say - everyone over the years can look from the bus and up close, and let the eye send its message - for me one of increasing delight.

What was the big idea? (The Victorians, as Simon Heffer has explained had "High Minds" which we must study if we wish to understand ourselves). The big idea was: power, progress and piety - depicted in ascending layers of sculpture, from the four continents at the base corners, through representations of trades & occupations, then moral virtues and spiritual virtues, to the cross at the apex - resembling the Eleanor Cross (in front of the Charing Cross Hotel).

EUROPE.

As we should expect Europe counted as the most important of the four continents, the central feminine figure holding a scepter and an orb. And the feminine figure rearest to us in the photograph, holding a trident in her right hand and a shield in her left, is obviously Britannia - or the Athena of "New Troy".

TRAJAN. Does he reflect the four cardinal virtues? What were they? How was Trajan connected with Christianity? How may he be compared to Aeneas? What connection can be made with the Boy Scouts, and with "If"?

TRAJAN

'The Roman Connection'

The bronze statue found in a Southanpton scrapyard in 1972 and presented to the nation by Toby Clayton now stands near Tower Bridge Underground Station in front of a fragment of Roman Wall. This illustrations, way might say, 'the Roman connection' which began around 50 A.D. with the founding of Londinium. It was followed by three other "glocal" events, to do with religion, culture and politics. Which were these?

Who was Trajan? Like Horatio Nelson, he was a truly well-loved warrior, and his column near Piazza Venezia in Rome was the model for Nelson's Column in Trafalgar Square in London. And as this marked the near peak of British imperial power, so Trajan's Column marked the summit of the Roman Empire, in 117 AD.

Not only - Trajan's Column was a masterpiece of Roman art, with the emperor's Dacian campaign sculpted on it in a narrative spiral of panels. This stood at the end of the Forum of Trajan, towering above two facing libraries, one for Greek and one for Latin volumes. In front of them, stretching across the Forum, was the magnificent Basilica Ulpia - twenty columns long by eight columns wide - Corinthian columns which supplied the precise sculptural model for Nelson's Column.

"Princeps Optimus"

Depicted on Trajan's Column were 2,500 figures involved in the Dacian Campaign: his army all engaged in different tasks - clearing woodland, building brides, etc. - the emperor himself among them, directing operations. Yet he was not only a good general who led from the front his "excellent and most loyal fellow soldiers" - he was also a courteous head of state who favoured open government. He systematized legal & fiscal procedures, and founded "alimenta" - financial provision for poor children.

His age was one in which the grandeur of Rome was enhanced - like London in the Regency and reign of George IV. - Constantine declared that Trajan's Forum was "the most exquisite structure under the canopy of heaven". Also, the idea of piazzas with colonnades came in, and the creation of a beautiful market - of which we can get an idea in Convent Garden. At the same time, it was a time of literary renaissance - with Tacitus, Pliny the Younger, Plutarch and Dio Chrysostom.

Justice and Pity.

Yet what is most admirable about Trajan was his sense of justice and pity, appreciated by Gregory the Great, which inspired the altar piece of Jaccopo Avanzi at the Pinacoteca di Bologna, triplych of the Fathers of the Church in Munich, and a bas-relief in the Supreme Court in Washington — all concerned with Justice.

The story goes that the emperor was about to ride from Rome with his army, according to Marcus Aurelius, when a poor and elderly widow, full of tears, clutched the horse's bridle and begned him for justice against the murderer of her son. Trajan answered that justice would be done on his return, but she would not loosen her grip, saying "And if you do not return?" "Then whosoever wears my crown will right the wrong", he replied, to which she responded, "And can the good deed another does grace and profit him who shows his own responsibility to do well?" At that, the emperor paused, dismounted, and announced, "Rest assured. It is clear to me that this duty is to be done before I leave. Justice calls me, pity binds me here."

Gregory the Great was so moved by the tale that he promptly prayed for intercession on Trajan's behalf ..: "Forgive, almighty God, the errors of Trajan, because he always maintained right and justice." The clouds parted and God, in his infinite Mystery and Wisdom, proclaimed, "I hear your petition and pardon Trajan ..." This created theological problems for the Church, but Dante in the end put Trajan among the Just and Temperate Rulers in the sixth sphere of the Paradiso.

Trajan and Aeneas (history & myth)

So we can see that the Roman statue not far from Tower Hill Underground represents a different soul from the other one by the gift shop, of Jack the Ripper. It represents a humane soul rather like the mythological hero of Virgil - the role model required by Augustus to inspire his empire. All three, in fact, had Stoic virtues - were sober, steady types who didn't give up (think of Kipling's "If").

The starting point for Augustus' spin poet was, of course, Homer's Iliad. His hero was a son of Priam, king of Troy who, just before Troy fell, was instructed by Poseidon to escape & found a new Troy on the banks of the Tiber.

Result: the picture of a new kind of hero - a family man plodding through the burning ruins with his father on his back and small son holding his hand, his wife somewhere behind him. Aeheas! Can you remember the hero of the Iliad - Achilles? How were they different?

Aeneas was more our kind of hero, whose task was long and complicated and unspectacular - hot quiak and glorious. Think of Afghanistan and Iraq.

Aeneas had first, like Odysseus, to make a long journey - as a displaced person - to a new land, to be Italy. Then, like Achilles, he had to fight in order to establish the new city. Any such enterprise in the ancient world required advise from an oracles and Aeneas went to Cumae to consult the Sybil: she instructed him to visit the Underworld. To do this he had to pluck the golden bough.

He learns from the priestess of Apollo that he will have to undergo much suffering and bloodshed. He responds to her question stoically:

"O Virgin Goddess, no suffering can be new; all I have known and felt deep in my heart".

The great man helped the poor,
    And poor men loved the great;
Then lands were fairly portioned:
    The spoils were fairly sold;
The Romans were like brothers
    In the brave days of odd."

This is, of course, an unfashionably idealised picture of Republican Rome- bat one largely shared by the Founding Fathers, and by Lord Byron who came to Rome in 1817. In any case, it inspired the young Winston, and the war leader of 1942 became enthusiastic when his friend Lord Birkenhead quoted the key lines of the Aenead to him:

"Your task, Romans, you must never forget,
will be to rule peoples imperially,
(these are your arts) to impose habits of peace,
spare the defeated and repress the proud"

To this he murmured that he might have said that himself and that he often arrived at the same conclusions as the Romans without their help. Towards the end of the war he told the Americans - then clearly emerging as the world power- that they must "think imperially" and play not merely a national role on the world's stage.

Women in love

Women obviously get the worst of it in wars. Even if they get killed, men may become heroes, while women risk losing husbands, lovers or sons - or being abandoned. The story, in Western literature, starts with Andromache's long good-bye to Hector at the gates of Troy - vainly she pleads with him not to leave her but to stay and fight inside the city walls. The baby Astyanax screams and shrinks into the nurse's breast, as if he knows what is in store...

It took Odysseus ten years to return to Ithaca from Troy but he did meet Calyso on the way (and Freud seems to after 17 years as Captain was rapidly promoted to lead the mobile column to capture Lucknow at the time of the Mutiny. His success was celebrated like that of Nelson, and his death, in London. He bade his men, as they assaulted Lucknow, to attend to their immortal souls.

Napier way less religious, but a radical, sympathetic to the Chartists whom he had to control in the north of England. He was "descended" from Charles II and a friend of the Duke, who asked him to go to India in the days of coming Mutiny. He ruthlessly annexed the Sind in 1843, but governed it afterwards with efficiency and justice- note present day politicians!

Unlike Havelock who died nobly in the heat of India, Napier returned to England as he had wished with enough money to pay for the education of his two handsome daughters by a Greek wife.

How many similar Roman figures are there in London, who served the Empire in India - incorruptible most of them, most speaking at least one native language, some like Lord Lawrence most close to and loved by Indians.

Man with a mission

"What is our aim? ... Victory, victory at all costs, victory in spite of all terror; victory, however long and hard the road may be, for without victory there is no survival."

These words, of course, were spoken in 1940 by the man whose statue faces Big Ben - Winston Churchill, clearly a man with a mission. (Observe his face, & hand gripping the stick.

As a boy in his nursery he would organise battles with hundreds of lead soldiers and play for hours on end. As a student at Harrow he won his only prize for reciting Horatius":

"Then none were for a party
Then all were for the state

have thought that Odysseus wasn't that keen on getting back to Penelope) - he met Calypso, but his time with her came to an end when Zeus's messenger, Hermes, came to tell him to move on. Poor Calypso! In the end, of course, Odysseus did get back to Ithaca and, with the help of Athena, kill the suitors and take Penelope in his arms. He was home at last...

For Aeneas it was a different matter. He, too, had problems in getting to his destination - which was not home but another place. He was a displaced person, after the destruction of Troy and, as he tramped out of the smoking ruins, carrying his father on his back and leading his small son Julus by the hand. he turned round to discover that his wife Creusa wasn't with them. He shouted "Creusa! Creusa!" but she had disappeared for ever.

What was Aeneas up to? Where was he going? What quality does he represent? Is he like Achilles, whose statue stands at Hyde Park Corner? No, Achilles represents Excellence -- the reward of which is glory, everlasting fame. That's it. Achilles was a loner. Aeneas, like Churchill, was a man with a mission- a long hard one. He was a man of destiny, who had to found "New Troy" on the banks of the Tiber.

But on the way he was shipwrecked on the coast of Dido Lybia, where the queen of Carthage Dido hosted him and, of course, it was rather like the case of Odysseus and Calypso. Venus, Aeneas's mother, and Juno, the quarrelling wife of Zeus, arranged for the two to shelter in a cave during a thunderstorm - and you don't need to be told what the thunder and lightning symbolizes.

A shattering blow for Dido

Can you guess what happened to Odysseus? What was Aeneas supposed to be doing? Jupiter, of course, soon learned what was happening in Carthage - and sent Mercury off with a message, to Aeneas, telling him he must be on his way - to found a New Troy.

What does he do? To leave or not to leave, that is not the question. He he has no choice - he is "Aeneas pius". What does "pius" mean? It does mean "pious", but also "dutiful", "committed" - a lot of things. Above all, obedience to the gods. (In what other ways was Aeneas dutiful?)

In this situation, Aeneas has no choice - so he starts making preparations to set sail, without telling Dido.

But Dido, of course, gets wind of this and expresses her feelings:

> "You traitor - did you imagine you could
> get away without a word, does our love
> mean nothing now? Or the prospect of me
> left all alone to die in misery?
> Why must you sail now on such stormy seas?
> Have you forgotten the promise you made?
> All I have given you with all my heart?
> I beg you, if it isn't too late, don't go!"
> Aeneas now remembered Jove's advice
> and didn't move his eyes; he struggled with
> the anguish in his heart; at last he spoke;
> "Dido, as long as I live I'll remember
> all you have done for me; it's hard to speak.
> I can only say I never intended
> to let you down or leave without a word.
> If the Fates left me free to live my life,
> I'd be most concerned about Troy and all
> my folk there who are living, and build

them a new citadel at Pergamon.

But now Apollo has commanded me

to lay claim to the land of Italy -

so his oracle says, and Italy

shall be my love and homeland..."

Under orders from the gods

When Aeneas met Dido in the Underworld, he could not look her in the face. How could he explain his behaviour? He had had no choice - he was under orders from the gods.

So Dido passed on, gazing at the ground, speechless. Aeneas was a man with a mission. Put unlike Winston Churchill he had no Clementine to comfort and support him. And whereas Winston's mission was to save Europe from the tyranny of Hitler, Aeneas mission was to plant the seed of European civilisation.

How? By founding the first settlement in Italy that would grow into an empire and establish around the shores of the Mediterranean cities on the Greek model.

This was promised by Jupiter. These Trojan migrants - Romans to be - "were set no boundaries in space or time ... (were) given rule without end". "So great a task it was to found the Roman nation."

But "the rule without end" was to mean the evolution of a new religion within the imperial system, In the words of Gibbon, "a pure hand humble religion gently insinuated itself into the minds of men, grew up in silence and ... finally erected the triumphant banner of the cross on the ruins of the Capitol." As we shall see, St Paul was able to exploit both the lingua franca, Greek, and the reads of the Roman Empire to spread the good news of Christianity. And he was free to do this as a Roman citizen, protected by Roman law.

Aeneas, the Stoic leader

AENEID I

'My friends, this is not the first trouble we have known. We have suffered worse before, and this will pass too. God will see to it. You have been to Scylla's cave and heard the mad dogs howling in the depths of it. You have even survived rocks thrown by the Cyclops. So summon up your courage once again. This is no time for gloom or fear. The day will come, perhaps, when it will give you pleasure to remember even this. Whatever chance may bring, however many hardships we suffer, we are making for Latium, where the Fates show us our place of rest. There it is the will of God that the kingdom of Troy shall rise again. Your task is to endure and save yourselves for better days.' These were his words, but he was sick with all his cares. 'He showed them the face of hope and kept his misery deep in his heart.

Their great ancestors of their mission

AENEID VI

'Now turn your eyes in this direction and look at this family of yours, your own Romans. Here is Caesar, and all the sons of Iulus about to come under the great vault of the sky. Here is the man who's coming you so often prophesied, here he is, Augustus Caesar, son of a god, the man who will bring back the golden years to the fields of Latium once ruled over by Saturn, and extend Rome's empire beyond the Indians and the Garamantes to a land beyond the stars...

'But who is this at a distance resplendent in his crown of olive and carrying holy emblems? I know that white hair and beard. This is the man who will found our city on laws ...Do you wish to see now the Tarquin kings, the proud spirit of avenging Brutus... He will be the first to be given authority as consul and the stern axes of that office. When his sons raise again the standards of war, it is their own father that will call them to account in the glorious name of liberty. He is not favoured by fortune, however future ages may judge these actions - love of his country will prevail with him and his limitless desire for glory....

Where are you rushing that weary spirit along to, you Fabii? You are the great Fabius Maximus, the one man who restores the state by delaying. Others, I do not doubt it, will beat bronze into figures that breathe more softly. Others will draw living likenesses out of marble.

Others will plead cases better or describe with their rod the courses of the stars across the sky and predict their risings.

Your task, Roman, and do not forget it, will be to govern the peoples of the world in your empire. These will be your arts - and to impose a settled pattern upon peace, to pardon the defeated and war down the proud.'

Horatio Nelson - the Character of an officer

Everyone must know the signal that Nelsom sent out to the navy before the Battle of Trafalgar in 1805, "England expects that every man will do his duty". Some will have noted that his first name is Roman - which is surely the key to his character.

"The character of an Officer is his greatest treasure: to lower that, is to wound him irreparably ... my character man will bear the strictest investigation. I stand for myself; no great connexion to support me if inclined to fall; therefore my good name as a Man, am Officer, and an Englishman, I must be very careful of. My greatest pride is to discharge my duty faithfully; my greatest ambition to receive approbation for my conduct." 12 Feb. 1796

On leaving Merton for the last time - "At half-past ten drov.my carriage from dear dear Mertom, where I left all which I hold dear in the world, to go to serve my King & Country. May the great God whom I adore enable me to fulfil the expectations of my Country; and if it is His good pleasure that I should return, my thanks will never cease being offered up to the Throne of His Mercy. If it is His good providence to cut short my days upon earth, I bow with the greatest submission, relying that He will protect those so dear to me, that I may leave behind. - His will be done: Amen, Amen, Amen." 13 Sept. 1805

MAHATMA GANDHI

His statue in Tavistock Square, is among the trees & frequently adorned with flowers. We may there in peace observe his rugged features, or gaze from the bus or pavement when walking from Russell Square to the British Library.

In sept 1903 a young Indian in white flannel suit arrived in Bayswater to look for lodgings. A law student with little money, porridge for breakfast & little else but bread. He pined for his mother, remembered her piety & injunction never to eat meat.

The young man now strove to become a gentleman: he paid ten pounds for a top hat, and had his gold watch and heavy gold chain sent out by his brother. He spent 20 minutes in front of the mirror in the morning; he took dancing lessons and learned French. But this phase lasted only three months, when he realised it was useless, though he had not yet reached the conclusion that the British Empire was bad and must be resisted.

But, most important, he made friends and was introduced to the Blaghata Gita in translation, and discovered the Sermon on the Mount. He mixed with people of different religions, & discovered, as Voltaire had done when drinking coffee at the Royal Exchange in 1727, that in here it was possible to meet people from everywhere, to talk & trade & barter freely.

All while he was graduating in law, and when this was achieved, he could dress and plead in the accepted way, having an insight into the mentality of his adversaries. It was, however, an important part of his training -- to feel the part of an opponent and be able to plead in the accepted style. As Gandhi struggled to get by, eating porridge for breakfast and little else but bread during the day, he remembered his mother always, and her warning to remain vegetarian.The Hindoo teaching of his parents remained strong in his heart, but he grew to appreciate not only the Blagatavita but above all the Sermon on the Mount. He continued a dialogue with Muslims.

When practising as a lawyer in South Africa, he came to the moment of decision: to fight against British imperialism. He discovered the key in 1910, with the so called Salt March, a nonviolent protest against the taxing of salt. You could break a regime, at least this less violent one, by passive resistance. This, of course, was the big lesson he passed on to Nelson Mandela.

ST PAUL (10 A.D. – 67A.D.)

Who notices the statue on a column near the Cathedral? We may notice the statue of Wesley when walking around the building to the left, and Wesley's finger is pointing up towards his mentor above him. It was Paul's words, commented on by Luther that inspired Wesley at Aldersgate in 1738: "I felt my heart was strangely warmed. I felt I did trust in Christ, Christ alone for salvation". It was the Letter to the Galatians that inspired Oliver Cromwell, and unnoticed on the Victoria Embankment, William Tyndale, translator of the Bible — was inspired by St Paul, through Luther at Wittenberg. He died in exile, strangled and burnt at the stake as a heretic — for wishing to give the Bible to all to read.

Who was this saint, so important in the history of Europe and the world? He was born in Tarsus, in present day Turkey in 10 A.D, raised as a Jew in a Jewish diaspora, with a training in Greek. He became a pharasee who persecuted Christians, who stoned the first Christian martyr, Stephen. But on the road to Damascus, in 36 A.D., he saw a vision of Christ, and was converted to the Faith.

After that Paul, as he now became known, made three enormous missionary journeys, from Antioch in Syria and moving westwards through modern day Turkey and Greece and finally back to Jerusalem again. This was heavy going for him as, unlike other early Christian missionaries, he had to earn his living wherever he went, making tents. His preaching of the Gospel was combined with the work of his hands. Paul's life changed the course of Christianity, turning it into a worldwide religion -- through his work as apostle, theologian, and letter-writer. His teaching concerned the Christian's relationship to Christ, hinging on justification through faith -- so that the Reformation of Martin Luther emphasized that the just live by faith - all they have to do is trust in the righteousness of God through Christ: "We have an advocate with the Father, Jesus Christ the righteous, & He is the propitiation for our sins".

This statue represents the third of the three journeys starting from present day Turkey and spanning the Mediterranean. There was, first, the visits by Homer to different islands in the Aegean and places on the coast of Turkey, second, the flight from Troy by Aeneas along a roundabout route ending in Rome and, third, the journeys between Tarsus, Jerusalem and Rome, on which Paul spread the Gospel of Christ. Three itineraries: one laying out the conceptual frame, one the social and one the spiritual

PREPARATION FOR A VISIT TO ROME

LORD BYRON & THE GRANDE TOUR.

Two years after Waterloo, Lord Byron arrived in Piazza di Spagna, where John Keats died, by the Spanish Steps. Poor Keats had little time left, and saw little in three months, except Napoleon's sexy sister, in the Villa Borghese. But Byron, like Shelley, did Italy as a Grand Tourist should, arriving in Rome via Venice and Florence. In three weeks he noted a tremendous number of things, explored the Roman Countryside on horseback, and wrote the fourth canto of "Childe Harold's Pilgrimage". Was he a pilgrim? Judge for yourself:

O Rome! my country ! city of the soul!
The orphans of the heart must turn to thee
Lone mother of dead empires!

Its obvious Byron felt at home here, while Goethe called Rome the "great school of the world". Amid the ruins, Madame de Stael imagined herself, as Corinne, with her lover, in a dialogue between the Mediterranean and the north; Sienkiewicz imagined the doors of the Mamertine prison screech open at sunset, and Peter stride forth. At Albano, Gogol pictured the mystery of creation emanating from a girl at a fountain, while an American Nathaniel Hawthorne, discovered Taste gazing at two huge statues in Piazza del Quirinale.

If one of these ideas is exciting, you have a guide, in Rome, or in the Campagna Romana outside Rome. And when in London, the columns, porticos, and churches may begin to look different, in Roman light so perhaps the Grand Tour isn't over. It's about what we see and the feelings we have, even if we come on a charter flight with a lap-top, not in a horse drawn carriage with servants.

2 FUNNY FEELINGS.

When we get to Rome, there's too much to see, and we don't know where to start. So it's natural to walk up and down, like the Londoner in the song:

"Maybe it's because I'm a Londoner
That I love London town,
I get a funny feeling inside of me
When walking up and down"

Why the funny feelings? This can be explained by experiments on the retina of the eye. Scientists say that the retina sends twelve films to the brain before the brain can compose a picture (one has to do with light and shade, another with movement — the others haven't been fathomed out). So John Ruskin was right, as usual, when he said " the eye is streets ahead of the brain "— and Goethe was right to trust his eye when he said: "I let the eye to get on with its work," and he urged us to do the same, to draw every day, noting every detail...

It seems likely that our eyes stimulate "funny feelings", when "walking up and down". And at the same time coordinate what we hear, smell, taste, or touch - so all five senses contribute to how we feel and what comes into our minds. And, sooner or later, if we feel passionate, these feelings can lead to dialogue & articulate knowledge.

Subsidiary & focal attention.

Funny feelings come when we're relaxed, in other words casually noticing many things, and not focusing on just one (Polayni distinguishes between subsidiary attention and focal attention). We may day-dream while glancing around at the panorama of Forum & Palatine under a deep blue sky, pine trees on horizon, and sea beyond, but sooner or later, one object will grip our attention. Then we gaze, perhaps at the Arch of Constantine. And while gazing, various ideas will come into our heads, and begin to group themselves together -- which is contemplation.

This ancient arch may remind us of the Marble Arch, which we have passed many times on the bus, but never studied. How many know this was modelled on the Arch of Constantine, and first stood in front of Buckingham Palace, designed by John Nash in 1828 & moved to Hyde Park in 1861? The Marble Arch must have been influenced by the victory at over the French at Wateroo, -- and be connected with the statues of Wellington, and maybe the cocksure, stylish, Palmerston in Parliament Square. His boast of 1850, "the sun never sets on the British Empire" is expressed in this arch.

But the Arch of Constantine celebrated the triumph of Christianity as religion of the Roman Empire, after the Battle of the Milvan Bridge in 313 A.D. Like photographs in the News of the World, the sculpted images on this arch touch on many aspects of life, centred on the two winged figures of Victory at the corners of the central arch. At the bottom, there are beaten enemies, & spoils, and half way up four medallions with river deities & hunting scenes; then panels showing assemblies of senators, and there are two faces of the emperor himself, recut from the heads of Trajan & Marcus Aurelius, showing how close he was to these two pagan goodies, his predecessors. (Dante tried to squeeze Trajan into Paradise, with a special recommendation to Gregory the Great).

Like most monuments in Rome, this is "conjunction of different civilisations through art" (an expression coined by an eminent

French visiter in 1727, Montesquieu, who otherwise slated the Vatican State for its various shortcomings). But here all the bits and pieces in the collage, plundered from other monuments, are pagan, though carefully chosen. Only the message is Christian, on the inscription, telling us Constantine was "instinctu divinitatis mentis magnitudine" -- "inspired by a god and the greatness of his mind" to triumph over a tyrant and serve the state. Like Homer's heroes, he needed both divine help, and his own ability.

The Romans often got divine help when it was needed. Before it came from the twin sons of Zeus, the horse tamers Castor and Pollux. They whizzed down from the sky to help the Romans beat the Latins at Lake Regilus in 499 B.C.. And now, just as in the First World War the angels of Mons appeared in the sky to inspire the allies, now the sign of the cross appeared in the sky to inspire Constantine. So he defeated Maxentius at the Battle of the Milvan Bridge. Constantine regarded this sign of the cross in the sky as a promise of divine support, and he became a convert to Christianity -- the first Roman emperor to be a Christian. Some say he was an opportunist, hedging his bets; some that he was truly converted to the Faith.

But as we gaze at the Arch of Constantine in Rome, under an azure sky, how do our memories of the Marble Arch colour our feelings, if at all? Memories of red buses, speeches at Hyde Park Corner, Christmas shopping in Oxford Street? If we ever noticed the figures of Victory on the Marble Arch, do they make the figures on the older arch look old and experienced? In fact this goddess of Victory meant a lot to the Romans and there was a real fuss when a later Emperor decreed her statue should be removed from the Senate (Curia) in 375 A.D. and the sacred flame in her temple extinquished. A bit like saying the torch to the unknown warrior should be put out. In any case, if we get funny feelings while gazing at the Arch of Constantine, they may in some slight way be influenced by memories of London centred on the Marble Arch.

The same may be said of all the porticos we see in London -- of the Royal Exchange, the National Gallery, the British Museum, which make the shape of the Pantheon portico familiar, with its eight massive Corinthian columns. How can we measure the effect of this portico, and of the dome inside? This was most perfect building of ancient times -- which inspired scores of porticos all over the world, not only London, and tremendous domes like those in the B.M. Reading Room and the Bank of England.

3 TIME LINE AND LIBERTY

When sorting out our funny feelings, it's a good idea to have a framework of dates, with important events,and figures.. Here is a skeleton framework, in five parts: Kings, Republic, Empire, Transition, and Christianity.

KINGS. Romulus, of course, was the first king of Rome (753 B.C.), and may be associated with the Ponte Rotto, site of the first wooden bridge across the Tiber, Pons Sublicius, the original junction of roads, trade routes and site of markets.

REPUBLIC. Brutus was the founder of the Republic (509 B.C.) which we associate with the Forum.

EMPIRE. Augustus was the founder of the Empire (27 B.C:), following the assassination of Julius Caesar. The universality of empire is suggested by the dome of the **Pantheon.**

TRANSITION. Constantine was the first Christian emperor, following his victory over Maxentius at the Battle of the Milvan Bridge in 313 A.D.E.. So his arch is a symbol of transition, but so is the **Colosseum** (80 A.D.) as here we imagine Christians dying for their faith, though the crucifiction of Christ took place earlier in 30 A.D., and those of Peter and Paul in 64 A.D., before its construction in 81 B.C.

CHRISTIANITY. St Peter was crucified in Rome in 64 A.D., as "the Rock" appointed by Christ. **St Peter's Basilica** was built here, first in 327 A.D., by Constantine, then the present building, largely designed by Michelangelo, was consecrated in 1626 (after 120 years' work).

PERIODS, MONUMENTS, DATES

KINGS	753 B.C. -- 509 B.C.	PONTE ROTTO
REPUBLIC	509 B.C. -- 27 B.C.	ROMAN FORUM
EMPIRE	27 B.C. - 476 A.D.	PANTHEON
TRANSITION	30 A.D. on	COLOSSEUM
CHRISTIANITY	313 A.D. on	ST PETER'S

Byron's comments on these five phases & monuments

Byron makes a wide sweep of history in "Childe Harold" after Greece, he touches on the Kings, Republic, Empire, of Rome, being inspired by particular spots, then the Transition to Christianity, and the triumph of the Faith but he is most interested in Liberty beginning in the Forum.

So it is a surprise, when we read

The Commonwealth of kings and men of Rome

but he had a soft spot for the second, most peaceful of Rome's kings, Numa Pompilius (rather like Edward the Confessor), and loved the idea of his nocturnal rendez vous with a nymph, Egea, who was supposed to give her lover divine hints on politics.

The **Roman Forum**, where the **Republic** grew up, focuses his political passion. Like the Founding Fathers of America, he discovered here the germs of democracy: the Curia was like a Senate or Lords, and the Comitium like a House of Deputies or Commons. But he had read the cynic Tacitus, and knew his hero Cicero was decapitated and his head exhibited here, with hacked off hands and tongue, so the Forum was for him:

The field of freedom, faction, feud and blood

Freedom, of course, was the big word for Byron, what he died for in Greece with a private multi-ethnic army, and what got him into trouble in Italy, for collaborating with an independence movement, the Carbonari.(Italy was still under French and Austrian rule). It was unusual for a Grand Tourist to be a political activist, who travelled all over Europe to discover what working conditions were like under different regimes. He was the Neruda of the time: he attacked Napoleon, and dictatorial rule in France, Greece, Spain & Portugal and was inspired by the example of democracy in America :

Yet Freedom! Yet thy banner, torn, but flying
Streams like the thunder-storm against the wind;
...
But the sap lasts, -- and still the seed we find
Sown deep, even in the bosom of the North..

The Pantheon seems to have represented Romanitas for Byron:

Simple, erect, severe, austere, sublime,
Shrine of all saints and temple of all gods,
From Jove to Jesus -- spared and blessed by time;
Looking tranquillity ...

And republican virtues, yet it was where globe-trotting Hadrian sat in council, the emperor whose eastern name was Zeus and western one Jove. With its dome it symbolizes **Empire** and universality.

The **Colosseum** was the building which most inspired Byron's sense of drama -- so the characters in Henry James' novel "What Maisie knew" went crazy about moonlight readings in the topmost seats of the Colosseum. And here Byron imagines the gladiator dying, (the

Dying Gaul in the Capitol Museum) when thousands are united with their emperor watching an act of courage and discipline which may even suggest the death of Christ himself:

> *I see before me the Gladiator lie;*
> *He leans upon his hand — his manly brow*
> *Consents to death, but conquers agony ...*

Finally, St Peter's profoundly inspires this romantic atheist. He records the feelings we have on entering only this church:

> *Enter: its grandeur overwhelms thee not;*
> *And why? It is not lessened; but thy mind,*
> *Expanded by the genius of the spot,*
> *Has grown colossal, ...*

4 ARE FUNNY FEELINGS SCIENTIFIC?

Surely, you may think, it isn't enough just to have funny feelings when you gaze at some statue or fountain, then remember the pleasure you when you get back home. Can this be scientific?

Three 'scientific criteria' are supplied by Michael Polyani, physical chemist turned professor of sociology: "certainty or accuracy", "systematic relevance", and "intrinsic interest".

What have these to do with funny feelings? Perhaps we can say, they supply a context for funny feelings, so we can see what importance they have.

My mental picture of the Temple of Castor & Pollux goes back to one July morning in the middle of the Roman Forum. I was contemplating the three tall marble columns, when I became aware of some-one behind me. This was a Japanese who discretely asked me where I was from. Hearing I was English, he quoted Shelley:

If winter is here, can spring be far behind?

This is, of course, a metaphor for contemplation -- a process culminating in a sudden key thought, after an apparently empty period. I don't know if he intended this, but his parting shot was: *we have to nourish contemplation.*

As I gazed at the three broken, patched up, weathered columns, held together by iron bands, I hadn't read about the archeologist's reconstruction: I didn't know these three columns were the only remaining ones on the east side of an octostyle temple eleven columns deep, measuring 39.50m X 50m, housing three cells, and podium, the office for weights & measures and bankers' stalls. I didn't know the temple was sometimes used as senate house where Cicero made some of his brilliant speeches, and Caesar spoke on the podium about agrarian reform.

I couldn't then connect these three columns with a complete building -- I was not immediately reminded of the portico of the National Gallery or the form of the Parthenon, as *I had no idea of the systematic relevance of these three columns to the original building..*

Why, then, did I stand there gazing, contemplating? Obviously, because *these columns had an intrinsic interest.* The surroundings, of course, were fascinating Forum, Palatine, deep blue sky, pines trees, wheeling birds, Etruscan Tabularium and, from close up, the surfaces of the ancient marble were fascinating -- worn and weathered, broken, chipped, patched up, held together by iron bands, wearing, in Ruskin's words, "the golden stain of time".

At the same time, I knew the story, doubtless disputed by historians, of how the twin sons of Zeus, once descended from the sky to help the Romans defeat the Latins at Lake Regillus in 499 B.C. Rather like the Angels of Mons who appeared to the allies in the First World War to inspire victory. The victory at Lake Regillus made the Romans masters of the peninsola, & the importance of this event is demonstrated by the huge equestrian statues in Piazza Campidoglio and Piazza del Quirinale. The latter are, maybe, the finest in Rome, and inspired the largest statue in London, of Achilles, in Hyde Park. (Though Shelley would not have gone into raptures about Achilles, as he did about the Castor & Pollux in Rome).

So, to sum up, the three columns had intrinsic interest for me because of their visual impact that day in their setting, & because of the importance of the legend about Castor and Pollux. Later, when I had studied different guide books, I could appreciate the certainty or accuracy represented by these three columns. I could understand their systematic relevance to the whole arrangement, in a rectangular temple eight columns wide and eleven columns deep. I could visualise the original complete building like the Parthenon, with a portico like that of the National Gallery or Pantheon (with eight columns).

This illustrates what Freud said, that Rome is a psychic space rather than a habitation, where each of us can reconstruct things as he or she wishes. Or, more simply, like children lost in wonder, we instinctively search for order. What other city presents so many challenges to the eye, intellect and imagination?

5 THE GOOD AND THE BEAUTIFUL

What is the meaning of beauty? When we see a photo of Kate Moss, do we think the Good and the Beautiful go together?

Three hundred years ago, the Earl of Shaftsbury thought they did -- and he was inspired by the figure of Virtue, resembling Athena. He was hooked on the Greek ideal of the Good and the Beautiful. He called this "Moral Sense".

But his ideas are a bit strange to us, as he thought only toffs could appreciate beauty, while the rest of us were capable of enjoying public executions at Tyburn (where twelve scaffolds operated simultaneously, and hangmen added daily to their collections of jackets and watches Charles Dickens' Barnaby Rudge).

But his idea took off, and his most popular work in 1711 ran into many editions. Philosophers on the Continent praised it, & wealthy families from all over Europe sent their sons with tutors on the Grand Tour. They wanted to turn their spoilt sons into "real fine gentlemen, ... such as have seen the world, and informed themselves of the manners and customs of the several nations of Europe, searched into their antiquaries and records, considered their police laws, and constitutions...architecture, sculpture, painting, music, ... poetry, learning and conversation."

Then, as regards the good and the beautiful, Shaftsbury preached "What is beautiful is harmonious and proportionable; what is harmonious and proportionable is true; and what is at once both beautiful and true is of consequence agreeable and good ..." So beauty makes us serene, gives us a sense of proportion & harmony, helps us to reconcile our own desires with those of others. It is, he believes, something natural, this "Moral Sense" and not the fruit of reason. Yet it requires a choice, between two ways of life.

His role model was Hercules who had to make a choice between Virtue and Pleasure, and chose "a life full of toil and hardship, under the conduct of Virture, or the deliverance of mankind from tyranny and oppression". She guided him "by her eloquence and other charms" and "made herself mistress of the heart of our enamoured hero.."

It is easy to understand this if we have been blessed with the help and advice of a wise tactful woman. (Emerson asked: "What is civilisation? The power of good women"). But what does his wonderful woman look like?

Shaftsbury had his ideas. He wrote that the statue of the goddess of Virtue had to be "a lady of goodly form, tall and majestic ... sufficiently accustomed to exercise", who might look like Athena, holding a spear or sword, and should be dressed neither carelessly nor beautifully.

When we look at the figure of Virtue in the niche at the left hand side of Neptune in the Fontana di Trevi, we see that she contrasts with Pleasure on the other side, who is a bit like Kate Moss -- alluring, attracting attention to herself. The Athena-like figure does not do this, but leads us somewhere, as it were, suggesting serenity and purpose. She will guide us if we choose, as Athena *offered* to guide Achilles at the beginning of the Iliad. There were severaò sides to Athena's character, as we shall see. Shaftsbury was emphasizing her most attractive side, as "the goddess of nearness", who can help us when we need help.

6 THE PROBLEMS OF EUROPE

The voice of Shaftsbury obviously belongs to another age, but when talking about "learning the customs and manners of the several nations of Europe" he is up to date --which suggests that the idea of Grand Tour isn't completely out of date.

Romano Prodi, writing about the problems of Europe in Il Mulino, pointed to a lack among member states of flexibility, solidarity, particular sensibility, give and take. In other words, a lack of human qualities, including knowledge of "the customs and manners of the several nations of Europe", and a lack of "Moral Sense" which includes "give and take" and "particular sensitivity". So Shaftsbury was saying some important things.

What is the EU doing to tackle these problems? The twinning of towns, and Erasmus projects, is aimed at making the people of one country familiar with the customs and habits of others, but Romano Prodi seems to be saying this isn't working -- that globalisation isn't working. If this is right, then glocality is the logical solution. In other words, individuals of different nations may be motivated to visit a place they love, instead of be directed by a bureaucratic organisation to to places they don't know. In other words, our so Grand Tour would take the form of life learning, through shared interests which converge on one place.

In this case, Franco Ferrarotti's hunch becomes very important: "in today's world, the Mediterranean is assuming a new central role, historical, economic and cultural. It is "becoming once again a cross roads as the dialectic between north and south, rich and poor, reexplodes." In this situation, " Italy will be able to demonstrate her historic stature and cultural maturity."

So Rome may have an important new role. If we instinctively turn to Rome as "the city of the soul", then a more inclusive version of the Grand Tour is a logical idea. So Rome, already a great tourist attraction, can become a place for personal discoveries and life learning that contributes to European unity. How? This question is the subject of the project.

7 THE DREAM OF ROME

The Dream of Rome is the response of a politician to the challenge of uniting Europe. While underlining the brutal side of ancient Rome, Boris Johnson marvels that many different peoples all wished to be Roman citizens.

Why? Augustus, helped by his spin poet, Virgil, managed to inspire devotion and respect while assuming ever more extensive powers, through various rituals and repetitions. All the five senses were involved in this process of creating a shared Roman identity. First, everyone enjoyed watching, with their emperor, the same engrossing spectacles in the Colosseum (even St Augustine had his arm twisted, and enjoyed it). This showed the world what Roman courage and discipline were, and inspired a sense of belonging to an exclusive caste defending its system against hooligans. Second, everyone could go to the public baths when they wished, not only for motives of health and cleanliness, but to enjoy different games and admire beautiful art. (The mayor, naturally, notes another loudly applauded activity that happened inside the baths). Third, everyone fingered the same coins and glanced daily at the same dandy image of the emperor, who focused political allegiance. Third, everyone spoke Latin and read Virgil, who brimmed with love of countryside, Roman customs and the deeds of a super cultural hero, Aeneas. Fourth, they splashed the same fish sauce, garum, over all their dishes (whereas in Brussels, everyone splashes their chips with an obstinately different sauce,). Fifth, like true Romans they used tweezers, to remove all unwanted hairs from the body. Sixth, they learnt to socialise in public loos and to pass the sponge. All these rituals or repetitions added up to a shared feeling of Romanitas.

What can we learn from all this? Clearly, there is no Augustus or Virgil around -- if Tony Blair became president of Europe, how could that smile convince Frenchmen, Poles, Germans, when Brits themselves are not impressed by it? As Johnson says, the most important ritual, watching the so called games in the Colosseum, is impossible to rival. Football matches and Song Contests are useless by comparison. We would need to roll into one the roars of Wembly Stadium, the blood of bull fights, the phantasy of Disney, the shivers of the Chamber of Horrors, the deference of the royal enclosure at Ascot, the spectacle of Bertram Mills' Circus, the horror of the electric chair, the cultural heroes of the National Gallery, the political atmosphere of Westminster, the statues of the British Museum. Then we might begin to capture the atmosphere in the Colosseum, as Byron has done in Childe Harold's Pilgrimage.

Boris Johnson bitterly regrets the ending of the Roman Empire. Though it is natural to regret the advantages of the empire, and to marvel at the union of physical health, culture and beauty that public baths encouraged, reading "Quo Vadis?" makes it hard to agree that Christians could have been more tolerant of such nasty emperors. In any case, when Rome was invaded by different peoples, it became, he says, like a chimpanzee's tea party, no-one knowing who was who. And as the prestige of the semi religious emperor faded and vanished, so did political allegiance, along with rituals and repetitions that make social cement.

Yet he reports one paradoxical sign of hope: in 417 A.D. a pagan poet, Rutilius Namantianus, paid Rome an incredible compliment, at a time when things were falling apart: "You have made out of diverse races one *patria*, one country". (What remained at the end of the British Empire --- the ideal of parliamentary democracy ?).

A similar compliment has been expressed right down the ages since, by illustrious visiters from different nations. We find it among the thoughts of Montaigne, the observations of Montesquieu, the thought world of Goethe, the sensitivity of Gogol, the perceptions of Stendhal,the democratic passion of Byron and Shelley, the faery stories of Hans Christian Andersen, the potent form of Ibsen, the lyricism of Lizst, the romanticism of Madame de Stael and Berlioz, the sensitivity of Hawthorne and political idealism of Margaret Fuller. All their works are inconceivable without their experience of Rome, which must have seeped through them into the hearts of their peoples.

Their fellow countrymen must have been affected by Rome, without knowing it -- though when they get to Rome they knew by instinct they belonged to the same universe of human feelings.These are embodied in sky, the countryside, piazza, life, manners and songs, architecture, music, sculpture and painting. Visiters feel at home and long to come back. Some talk about Rome as a kind of school. This universe of feelings is celebrated by Byron, Goethe, de Stael, Sienkiewicz, Gogol, Andersen, Hawthorne & Fuller, which makes their works important for rediscovering European unity.

This belonging to the same universe of feelings fits in with what Boris Johnson calls an unconscious allegiance to Rome, invisible like the subterranean wen of Roman drains and vaults and chambers that lies below the ground in all countries once ruled by Rome. So there is work to be done, building above ground, as if reconstructing a complete systems of Aquaducts converging on Rome, starting from the beautiful fragments we see can actually see. We know the rest exists, in the blood..

Yet some tourists today come out with not only beautiful fragments, but key thoughts, like those expressed by Grand Tourists. It is not true, what Roger Scruton says, that "High Culture" divides those who understand it from those who don't. Not only egg heads fall in love with Rome, like "orphans of the heart". Low brows also do -- who never gazed with Mum and Dad, like Goethe, at engravings of Piazza del Populo & statuettes of Apollo. Goethe's Dad sang Italian songs and wrote a book about Italy. No wonder he felt at home here.

Later we can discuss each visiter's thought or discovery separately -- here we may simply note their words and and the Grand Tourists who said the same thing.

A young Englishman in the bookshop by the Tiber Island murmurs what Byron exclaimed: "I feel kind of at home here"; a Canadian, like Goethe, in the same place, observes: "There's so much to learn, I'll always come back"; a Manchester lady on the bus with her friend at the Stazone Termine , like Madame de Stael, tells me as we pass the fragment of Servian Wall: "It's a lovely city, we feel safe here"; an Australian doctor, sitting on the parapet at sunset in Piazza del Quirinale with his wife and gazing at St Peter's, like Stendhal repeats, "I've never seen anything like it in my life"; a Saudi Arabian girl, in the Caffé Greco, speaking of the Pantheon, beams like Hans Christian Andersen, "I feel happy here"; a Paskistani lady in the Caffé Greco, like Gogol, sighs "My soul existed in Rome before I was born"; an American attorney, in the Caffé Greco, like Stendhal exclaims "There's excitement in the air, that's why I come back to Rome"; a young man from Arizona, in a bar at Frascati, like Shelley exclaims, "I want to die in Rome".

These thoughts have been far more fully expressed by Grand Tourists - but that doesn't matter: they represent the personal discoveries of different people who are now tip-toe-ing into the same universe of feelings which we call Rome. Their enthusiasm suggests that " a stumbling discovery is a finer thing than a well rehearsed tour." (Polanyni).

This is tacit knowledge, which intellectual passion may later turn into articulate knowledge, or else it will remain a precious secret we only trust to old friends.

The author of "The Dream of Rome" may reply, these are isolated cases, which have little to do with shared identity. True, but beneath the surface there is a sense of the same identity, beginning to surface among some who come to Rome. Their feelings are barely articulate, probably felt to be only "personal opinions". But with encouragement, they can be shared, compared with others and become articulate.

This process can be fostered in groups of friends.Then European unity can start among friends in the office or pub who like the idea of going to Rome. The first stage of a life learning process...

8 MICHELANGELO -- THE LAST WORD

Everyone who comes to Rome has the same thought sooner or later: those Romans were brutal so and so's, how is it possible Rome is such a lovely city?

But perhaps there's no problem. Michelangelo found himself one evening in the Colosseum in a snowstorm -- but he stayed, to contemplate the beauties of the building.He knew what he was doing, being obsessed with the task of building St Peter's. As Ibsen admired St Peter's, saying he now knew what he had to achieve -- "clear potent form", so Michelangelo must have had the same thought, contemplating the Colosseum. Here he could see clear potent form, which he wished to achieve in the design of St Peter's, much of it constructed with stone from the Colosseum. So here the "conjunction of different civilisations through art" happened on two levels -- of design and of material. (For this reason talks of "Christians" as well as "Goth" and "Fire" and "Flood" as destroying Rome)

In any case, for Michelangelo it was not the uses of the Colossem that mattered, but its beauty.He knew that he had to assimilate. Herder, the teacher of Goethe, stressed Rome's great capacity for assimilating the "maximum perfections of other peoples". The Romans had done this. Each of the other peoples they had contact with, had their glaring faults, but Rome knew how to take the best from each: from the Egyptians measurement and command of huge masses, from the Etruscans a sense of the sacred and engineering, from the Phoenicians, seafaring and commerce, from the Jews, piety and patriarchal values, from the Greeks beauty and liberty.

So the big question is, what can we learn in Rome? For the architect, the answer is clear: draw what attracts you, and find out. And this was the practical advice of Goethe to everyone: draw every day, however badly, to improve your powers of observation. And before you go back to the work you have taken a fancy to, find out more about it, as if it were a boy or girl you love. Study photos and diagrams, compare it with other works, discuss it with friends, study guide books, pester as many experts as you can. Make notes.

Goethe also said that every me was really several selves --- me and several other persons inside us -- influencing, guiding, all the time.

Where Rome is concerned, there are many guides to choose from, each offering different kinds of advice, as we have seen: Byron with an uncanny sense of place and history, Goethe with his insistence on the eye and on form and development of forms, Madame e Stael with her contrasting of Nordic & Mediterranean temperaments, Sienkiewicz with his sense of spiritual epic, Gogol with a more intimate contact, art as prayer, and Hawthorne with his American discovery of aestheic taste in the presence of masterpieces.

Empire - a warning to everyone. We see on the arch what happens to the enemies of Rome! Whereas the Marble Arch must have been inspired by memories of beating Napoleon at Waterloo, the Arch of Constantine celebrates the triumph of Christianity as the religion of the Roman Empire, after Constantine beat Maxentius at the Milvan Bridge in 312 A.D.

How much does the Marble Arch influence our feelings in front of the Arch of Constantine? This depends on how much well we know John Nash's work, but it must supply us with the general shape, & so enable us to concentrate better on the beautiful surface and details of the Roman work, a patchwork of pieces stolen from pagan buildings and fused into one Christian one. "Conjunction of different civilisations through art" (Montesquieu).

We may ask if other memories of London influence our funny feelings in Rome - for example, if St Peter's is influenced by memories of St Paul's, the Colonna Traiana by Nelson's Column, the Ponte Rotto, "Broken Bridge" by London Bridge?

There are at least two considerations: appearance, and historical analogy. St Paul's resembles St Peter's, so it should make the dome and bell towers of St Peter's familiar when we see them, and for those who remember how the dome of St Paul's survived the bombs of Hitler and gave hope to Londoners during the Blitz, it should add a whiff of nostalgia to our feelings in St Peter's Square. Nelson's Column represents the country's best loved warrior as well as one of the city's most familiar landmarks, so these feelings of patriotism could colour

our viewing of the Colonna Traiana, dedicated to Rome's best loved emperor. Yet we don't see the millionaire emperor Trajan at the top of the column depicting his feats of organisation during the campaign against the Dacians. Instead, we see a crude fisherman holding the keys of heaven. This is another example of what Montesquieu called "a conjunction of different civilisations through art". Something classical & pagan part is fused with something Christian.

Where the two bridges are concerned, it more a question of history than appearance : London Bridge is modern & functional, while Ponte Rotto is ancient and in ruins. But there is an analogy between "Broken Bridge" and "London Bridge is falling down". Both bridges have played a similar role in the history of the two cities when invaded. The hacking down of the Pons Sublicius, while Horatius fought off the enemy, prevented the Etruscan invasion of Rome in 510 B.C., while the pulling down of London Bridge prevented the invasion of the city by the Danes in 1000 A.D. So memories "London is falling down!" may colour our feelings as we view Rome's oldest bridge across the Tiber. This is where the city was born.

All the neo-classical porticos we see in London -- the Royal Exchange, National Gallery, and others, most with eight Corinthian columns, the Mansion House with six, may contribute to our viewing of the Pantheon in Rome, whose portico with eight Corinthian columns goes back to 118 B.C. Here we can focus attention on the capitals and weathered surfaces, wearing "the golden stain of time," before standing beneath the great dome, the mother of all other domes in the world, where Rome's most Hellenic emperor, Hadrian, received his advisers, & Raphael came to sit and draw.

The process of learning was for Goethe, the great German poet, a matter of returning constantly to the things you love. Between visits, you need to study, and pick the brains of as many experts as possible. That is why he called Rome "the great school of the world".

TIME LINE GROWTH OF INSTITUTIONS & LIBERTY

We need a time framework to fit our discoveries into. We may associate each key phase or aspect of history with particular monument:

Kings — Ponte Rotto	*Romulus 753 B.C. —*
	Tarquin the Proud, 710 B.C.
Republic — Forum	*509 B.C. to 55 B.C.*
Empire — Pantheon	*56 B.C 430 A.D.*
Transition — Colosseum	*100 A.D. to 312 A.D.*
Christianity — St Peter's	*312 A.D. onwards*

Kings — Ponte Rotto may remind us of Kings, starting with Romulus & the founding of Rome in 753 B.C, at a junction of roads, where there was the first cattle and vegetable market in Rome. Later, in 510 B.C., Horatius defended the bridge against the invading Etruscans, allied to Tarquin the proud, the last king of Rome. The image of the bridge collapsing before he jumped into the Tiber to swim to the bank may suggest "London Bridge is falling down".

The Republic -- Roman Forum is where all the activities of the Republic took place, for Byron:

"The field of freedom, faction, feud and blood"

and dear to the Founding Fathers of America, as here they could contemplate the Curia and Comitium, the oldest examples of Senate & House of Representatives in European history, two essential institutions to be copied.

The Empire — the **Pantheon**, with its massive dome, designed by Hadrian in 100 B.C. suggests universality and the unity of the Empire. Here the emperor Hadrian actually held court, and where there once stood statues of the twelve gods, before 600 AD. when the building was consecrated at a church, St Mary of the Martyrs. It was for Shelley, "the visible symbol of the universe".

Transition — the **Colisseum**, erected for games in 79 A.D., is a symbol of transition from classical paganism to as here we imagine Chrisitians dying for their Faith before crowd of Romans under their emperor. These terrible events are described in Quo Vadis? Then the magic of history is captured by Byron in describing this place by moonlight.

Christianity — **St Peter's** is of course, the emblem of the triumph of Christianity in Rome, constructed with marble plundered from different pagan classical buildings, above all the Colosseum. Paradoxically an atheist romantic, Lord Byron, best sums up the experience of entering this great building:

Enter; its grandeur overwhelms thee not,
But why? It is not lessen'd, but thy mind,
 Expanded by the genius of the spot
Has grown enormous...

ARE FUNNY FEELINGS SCIENTIFIC?

How, you may ask, can "funny feelings" be scientific? It can't be just a matter of what we feel in one place, and happen to remember when we get back home. How is it possible to make head or tail out of the Roman Forum, with millions of fragments, or rather just one object we find there? (far more difficult than groping our way among the muddle of monuments inside Westminster Abbey).

The key is supplied by Michael Polyani: science thrives on three factors: "certainty or accuracy", "systematic relevance" and "intrinsic interest." We have to take into consideration these three things.

My memories of the Temple of Castor & Pollux centre on a meeting two years ago with a Japanese scholar. While I was contemplating the three highest columns in the centre of the Roman Forum, I became aware of some-one standing behind me. Then he approached and discretely asked where I was from. Hearing I was English, he quoted Shelley: "If winter is here, can spring be far behind?" This line is a metaphor for contemplation, which bears fruit after a period in which nothing seems to be happening. I don't know if my Japanese friend realised this, but he concluded by saying, we must nurture contemplation.

In any case, I was contemplating the three tall marble columns in the centre of the Forum, weathered, patched up, chipped and held together by iron bands. I have since learned that these are three remaining columns on the east side of a complete octostyle temple eleven columns deep, about 30m wide and 50m long, like the Parthenon. It had a podium and three cells, housed the system of weights and measures, and was used at times as senate house. Caesar spoke from the podium on agrarian legislation, and Cicero here addressed the Senate.

But I did not, first of all, appreciate the systematic relevance of these three columns, starting with the "certainty or accuracy" they represent. I just felt their "intrinsic interest".

This "intrinsic interest" came through gazing at the deep blue sky, the wheeling of gulls, pine trees, horizon, massive Etruscan Capitol high up at the end of the Via Sacra, and remembering the legendary story which gives these three columns their historic importance. However debatable it is as history, the story of the twin sons of Zeus helping the Romans defeat the Latins at the Battle of Lake Regulus in 499 B.C., seems to have great importance for Rome. There are two huge monuments to Castor & Pollux in the city, one in Piazza Quirinale, and one in Piazza del Campidoglio. These four statues are the largest in Rome, and the ones in Piazza del Quirinale are surely the finest. (Shelley thought so, though he would not have been so ecstatic about the figure of Achilles in Hyde Park, the largest statue in London, modelled on one of the equestrian statues in Rome).

These giant figures reflect the historic importance of the legend and must have influenced me as I gazed at the "Temple of Castor & Pollux" that sunny morning in July. **So the columns aroused an intrinsic interest, before I had any idea of their systematic relevance based on certainty or accuracy.** Only after studying the guidebook could I reconstruct the whole building in my mind and imagine it as a place of cult, a room housing the system of weights and measures, and senate house, where Caesar spoke, and Cicero made great orations. Since then, of course, these three columns have become more significant, as I can imagine them as part of a complete temple like the Parthenon or a portico like the National Gallery in Trafalgar Square.

In the first place, however, I could not begin to do this, and did not wish to. My romantic imagination was content with three weathered, chipped, patched up marble columns, silhouetted against the deep blue sky of Rome, and wearing, "the golden stain of time" (Ruskin).

Freud called Rome a psychic space, not a place of habitation, where everyone could reconstruct monuments or ruins as they liked, making use of as much knowledge as they possessed. This is, of course, a never ending process & surely the biggest fascination of Rome -- a challenge to eye, logic, knowledge and imagination.

THE GOOD & THE BEAUTIFUL

What importance has beauty today? What message does Kate Moss project? Do her photos suggest to us both beauty and good? At the end of the Eighteenth century, the Earl of Shaftsbury thought beauty was strictly connected with good. He was hooked on the Greek ideal of the Good and the Beautiful.

The problem is, he belonged to a world of toffs: beauty for him was for "fine gentlemen" and not for ordinary mortals -- he thought most people were capable of enjoying only public executions at Tyburn, but not beautiful sculptures at the Fontana di Trevi in Rome.

But his big idea caught on, and many wealthy families of Europe sent their sons on a Grand Tour. They thought they could improve their career prospects, by discovering the Good and the Beautiful. The Grand Tour changed the face of Europe. Today, 70% of London's architecture is classical.

Architecture, you may retort, is only the one visible result. Yet his big idea, Moral Sense, impressed the great minds of the age, Herder, Leibniz, Montesquieu, & Diderot. Moral Sense, combining the good and the beautiful, derived from reason AND feeling, and aimed at reconciling private with public good. Though a Christian, Shaftsbury was inspired by Athena, as the goddess of Virtue, (in the niche to the right of Juppiter in the Fontana di Trevi). She inspired you to work for a better world, while Pleasure, in the opposite niche encouraged you to live it up.

His big work, "Concerning Virtue and Merit ran into 11 editions in 1711, and inspired rich families in many countries to send their sons with a tutor to "do" Europe, on a tour ending up in Rome.

The Grand Tour

The Grand Tour was a kind of finishing school. It aimed, like Castiglione's "The Prince" at training public servants. The idea was to learn "the manners and customs of the several nations of Europe, ... their principle arts, studies ... architecture, sculpture, painting, music, and their taste in poetry, learning and conversation"" .And as Greece and Rome was supposed to have the top models of beauty, Rome was a must, where you could be thrilled by beauty and discover what Moral Sense was. In Shaftsbury's words "What is beautiful is harmonious and proportionable ... (and) true ... and what is at once beautiful and true is... agreeable and good". In other words, Beauty is good for you: makes you serene and balanced and able to reconcile the private with the public good. And this process involved conversation in small groups of friends -- with "fine gentlemen" of course.

The goddess of Virtue

But it wasn't just a matter of snob sight-seeing. You had to make a choice: between Pleasure and Virtue. In "The Choice of Hercules", Shaftsbury urges us to choose "a life full of toil and hardship, under the conduct of Virtue," in order to save"mankind from tyranny and oppression". We can be inspired by Virtue herself "who by her eloquence and other charms has ere this made herself mistress of our enamoured hero". We can contemplate his Goddess of Virtue, in the niche on the right of Jupiter at the Fontana di Trevi, opposite the goddess of Pleasure on the left. This figure resembles Athene, "dressed neither negligently, nor with much study or ornament ... in her hand the imperial sword or spear" How does she compare with Kate Moss, on the pages of "Lite", or does Kate Moss more resemble the goddess of Pleasure?

THE PROBLEMS OF EUROPE

The words of Shaftsbury belong to a different world from ours. But the EU has aims rather like his. It aims, through the twinning of towns, to teach people in his words : "the manners and customs of the different nations of Europe", and Erasmus programs have similar aims for students, to be achieved through exchange visits between different universities.

The difference is, of course, a that the EU operates democratic system of brief exchanges, whereas Grand Tourists had plenty of time and money so they could spend a two year or two touring European cities and especially Rome. (Lord Burlington in 1782 brought 17 servants with him to Rome, including a barber; he had over 900 items of luggage including pencils & paper, pistols, prayer book and inflatable bath).

What success is the EU having? Romano Prodi, writing in Il Mulino last year, concludes that the problems of the EU are due to lack of "solidarity", "flexibility", "resourcefulness", "particular sensibility"-in other words, a lack of human qualities which we may consider were included in Shaftsbury's Virtue, or Moral Sense, which he said required "toil and hardship".

So if Shaftsbury's "Virtue" or "Moral Sense" included "solidarity", "flexibility", "resourcefulness" and "particular sensibility" (and we shall later think about Lord Palmerston as a model success story, fiercely criticized by Gadstone) it is relevant for Europe today. But it needs, of course, to be more inclusive, applying to sensitive people who may not be toffs.

At the same time, if Romano Prodi means that globalisation is not working, then glocality may be the answer. In other words, individuals, not bureaucratic organizations, keep visiting a place they love, where they can extend their horizons and understanding of other peoples. For this purpose, Rome has a lot to recommend it. Henry James discovered in Rome a "harmonizing charm". Though he was a bit of a snob, he praised Rome as he thought that all were nothing in Rome, and so equal. As we shall see, many others have had similar ideas, but visits to Rome require a strategy and preparation.

In conclusion, Prof.Franco Ferrarotti thinks that Mediteranean countries, Italy included, are "assuming a new central role in the world of today" to bring north and south, rich and poor countries together. So a great tourist attraction, Rome, may become an important meeting point, for improving international relations and uniting Europe, through exploiting a shared love of Rome.

THE DREAM OF ROME

"The Dream of Rome" was born as the response of a politician to the challenge of uniting Europe. Boris Johnson is inspired by the way ancient Rome united the countries of Europe, who today are disunited.. He emphasizes the brutal side of Romans, but marvels at how all peoples wished to be Roman citizens. How? Above all, he says, by craning their necks in the Colisseum, to watch in their thousands with their emperor those terrible spectacles of discipline and courage, then by fingering the same coins showing the head of Augustus, by reading Vergil and speaking Latin, by smothering all dishes with the same foul smelling fish sauce, by learning the use of tweezers to remove unwanted hairs, and by knowing how to pass the sponge in public loos. So they built up, through the five senses, a shared sense of identity, which we Eurovision song contests don't supply.

For Boris Johnson it was a disaster when the end came: when the barbarians arrived, and made up "a chimpanzees party" with Romans, no-one understanding who was who. And when, with Christianity, loyalty to Roman emperor & culture waned and with it a social cement.

Yet he supplies a hopeful sequel, with the story of the Barbarian poet, Rutilius Ramantianus, who declared "You have made a city out of what was once the world". That was in 417 A.D. -- and ever since similar thoughts have been echoed by great figures from different countries, who have come to Rome, been changed by Rome and changed their fellow countrymen in consequence.

This is shown in the reflections of Montaigne, the observations of Montesquieu, the thought world of Goethe, the romanticism of

Madame de Stael, the unforgettable words of Stendhal, the human sensitivity of Gogol, the faery stories of Hans Christian Andersen, the liberal idealism of Byron and Shelley, the epic grandeur of faith in "Quo Vadis?", the phantasy of Berlioz, the limpid form of Ibsen, the lyricism of Lizst, the artistic sensitivity of Hawthorne. So France, Germany, Russia, Poland, Norway, Denmark, Britain & America have all been nourished by works which grew out of the studied experience of Rome.

It is being in Rome, which counts, and which "The Dream of Rome" points to. Even today -- in a world of charter flights, package tours & brilliantly researched guides -- we can hear words which represent dimly but surely the unique universe of feelings which Rome represents and engenders -- words which slip out unnoticed. Not the feelings of Grand Tourists, but of "sensitive travellers". Where Rome is concerned, it is not quite true (as Roger Scuton argues) that "high culture" can be appreciated only by some.

The eight "travellers' tales" which follow all touch "High culture" indicating a love or need of the soul: "I feel kind of at home here", "There's so much to learn, I 'll always come back", "It's a lovely city, we feel safe here", "I've never seen anything like it", "I feel happy here", "I think my soul existed in Rome before I was born", "There's excitement in the air", "I want to die in Rome".

These comments reflect "funny feelings", stirrings of the soul, showing that people of different nations back up what Rutilius Namantianus in 417 A.D, said about Rome creating one city out of the world. They sum up in a crude way most of what Grand Tourists said about their experiences in Rome.

But as we shall see, case by case, the speakers were not very sure of what they were saying, imagining perhaps that these were "personal opinions " of little importance, or of little importance in a world of commerce & tehnology. These are mere, isolated words, our Mayor may say, not actual acts of shared enthusiasm, of political loyalty, of identical tastes, or intimate sensations of touch and smell. Yet they do represent intimate human feelings, of great importance, experienced, if not fully & consciously shared, by persons from all nations. They were, without knowing it, united by the subterranean streams of Rome that irrigate their cultures.

So the Dream of Rome is a challenge: to distinguish and magnify our childlike feelings of wonder, understanding instinctively guided towards an inner order we know what is happening and that others are doing the same.

Michelangelo -- the last word

The Dream of Rome throws up a contradiction, which must come into everyone's mind: these Romans were cruel bastards, but they created a lovely city. How can we reconcile the two aspects?

Perhaps it isn't necessary. Michelangelo visited the Colisseum one wintry evening. In spite of the driving snow storm, he was there to admire, and learn his trade. He had not come to reflect on the terrible spectacles, watched even by St Augustine, who had his arm twisted by his mates to go to the "games". What mattered to Michelangelo about this enormous building was "not its uses but its beauty."

The structural clarity and harmony of his new work, St Peter's, which so inspired Ibsen, was to grow out of the Colisseum. Surely this is a lesson in assimilation: concentrate on what you admire. "Cleave to that thou lovest" (Ezra Pound).

Herder stressed the imperfections of all the peoples which the Romans had learnt from: the Egyptians, Etruscans, Phoenicians, Jews, and Greeks. They all had their weaknesses, but the Romans, with their sixth sense of assimilation, learned something important from each of them: from the Egyptians, measurement and management of enormous masses; from the Etruscans, sacredness and engineering; from the Phoenicians, exploration and commerce; from the Jews, piety and patriarchal respect; from the Greeks, beauty and liberty.

Today what can we learn from the Romans, or rather from Rome? This is a difficult yet easy question. Difficult, as in Rome we get lost for words -- sensing things which are too hard to express. Easy, as it is a question of being human, as all the quoted persons imply. Each individual is more or less like a small child in love with his or her surroundings, and seeking a kind of order, which has nothing to do with the credit crunch or the war in Afghanistan. It requires cool to move with it, as the inner voice directs.

As an author and on behalf of my father Mr Day,
I would like to acknowledge and thank everyone
involved in the completion of this book.

The head of production: Luna Harrington together with
Mira Butler. Cover designer Anna Aleria and Rochelle
Mensidor, the interior layout designer, as well as Luke
Parker who regularly kept up to date with all liaisons.

They all made a great team and without an amazing
team, this project could not be completed.

Also, let us not forget the Universe, God , Spirit who in it's
strange way brought us all together and all readers.

Thank you from dad, wherever he is and myself, with
complete gratitude. May everyone be blessed always.

www.ingramcontent.com/pod-product-compliance
Lightning Source LLC
Chambersburg PA
CBHW021131130626
46554CB00002B/954

* 9 7 8 1 9 6 8 6 6 7 6 0 3 *